MALIA

AMNISSOS - NIROU KHANI
SKOTINO
CHERSONESSOS

ISBN 960-7310-85-3

COPYRIGHT:	I. MATHIOULAKIS & CO
ADDRESS:	ANDROMEDAS 1 ATHENS 16231
	TEL. 7661351 - 7227229
TRANSLATOR:	THANASIS HADZINICOLAOU
PHOTOS:	G. XYLOURIS

MALIA

AMNISSOS - NIROU KHANI SKOTINO CHERSONESSOS

ANTONIS S. VASSILAKIS
Archaeologist

ATHENS

ΑΝΤΙΠΡΟΣΩΠΟΣ ΚΡΗΤΗΣ
ΚΡΗΤΙΚΟ ΠΡΑΚΤΟΡΕΙΟ ΔΙΑΝΟΜΩΝ Ε.Π.Ε.
715 00 ΕΣΤΑΥΡΩΜΕΝΟΣ - ΗΡΑΚΛΕΙΟ
ΤΗΛ. 081 - 251.217

INDEX

INTRODUCTION

The northern coast of central Crete represents today the island's most touristic developed part with hundreds of hotels stretching from the Karteros Valley (the ancient river Amnissos or Triton), east of Heraclion to the shores of Milatos.

This coastal zone was densely inhabited throughout the antiquity. The harbours along the coast were used for Cretan trade while this zone constituted, as it does today, the natural gateway between central northern Crete (Knossos) and Eastern Crete (Gournia, Mochlo, Zakros). Halfway was the Minoan Palace of Malia.

On this coastal zone, the visitor may see a Minoan villa at **Amnissos** a Minoan mansion at **Nirou Khani,** three Minoan harbours at **Amnissos, Aghii Theodori,** near Nirou Khani and Malia. There is also the site at Malia including the Minoan Palace, the city and its cemeteries. Further, in the same area are the two sanctuaries, the Cave of Eileithyia at **Amnissos**, and the Cave at **Skotino.** In addition, the temple of the historic period dedicated to Zeus Thenatas, at **Amnissos,** as well as three Paleochristian Basilicae and a Roman theatre at **Chersonessos** may be visited.

All these ancient sites are along the main road with the exception of the cave at Skotino which lies at a distance of 5 kms. In our tour, we will visit the sites from west to east: Heraclion, Poros, Katsambas, Amnissos, Prassas, Nirou Khani, Gournes, Skotino, Chersonessos, Malia Milatos. The suggested tour is a full day excursion it can, nevertheless, be undertaken within halfday for those with limited time.

POROS - KATSAMBAS

Poros and Katsambas lie on the eastern outskirts of Heraclion. Katsambas is the name of the ancient river **Kairatos** which flows from Archanes along the Palace at Knossos to the Poros area. The archaeological finds in the estuary area are important due to the fact the here was the site of the city and harbour of Knossos. In the last twenty years the archaeologists K. Lembesis, A. Vasilakis and N. Dimopoulou have excavated in **Poros** large cave tombs dating from the first neopalatial period (1700-1500 BC).

These tombs comprised collumns, benches and depositors "bothroi" while the deceased were lain on wooden litters. Among the funeral presents found, hundreds of clay vases, gold and silver jewelry, seals, and necklaces of semi-precious stones stand out.

On the site of Heraclion's port were the harbour installations and dockyards of the Minoan period, known as **Trypiti.**

The most ancient ruins at **Katsambas** belong to a neolithic settlement, which was excavated by St. Alexiou some 30 years ago on a hillock west of the Department of Agriculture. A neolithic house as well as ruins of others were brought to light along an enclosure and eight courts and rooms containing stone tools, axes, millstones, whetting stones made of obsidian and flint, clay pottery dating from the mid-neolithic period (4500-3500 B.C.).

On the eastern slopes of the same hillock a large cemetery with chambertombs hewn in the rock and dating from the last part of the neopalatial and metapalatial periods has excavated. Here also the deceased were buried on wooden litters and among the funeral presents found, a number of wonderful vases (prochoi for libations) a pyxis made of ivory with a carved representation of the capture of a bull as well as some important Egyptian stone pottery stand out.

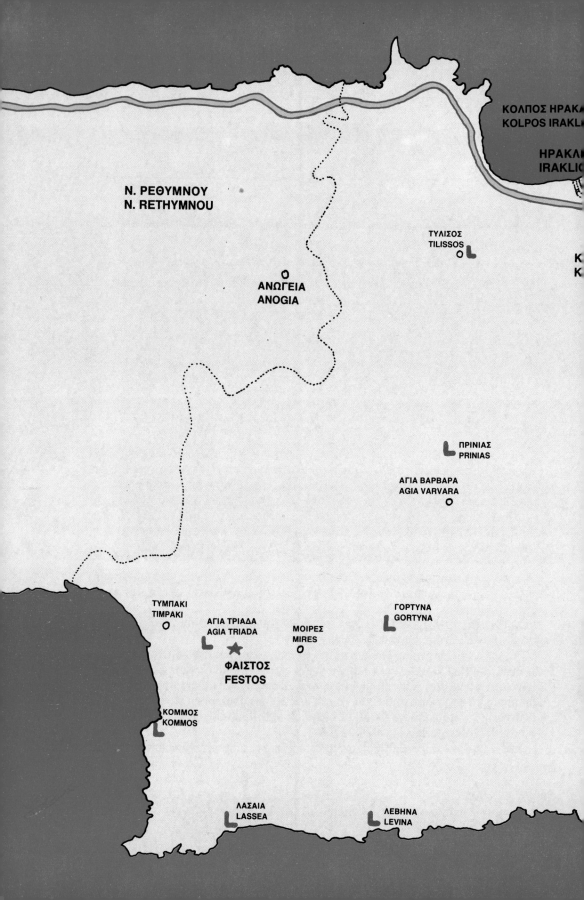

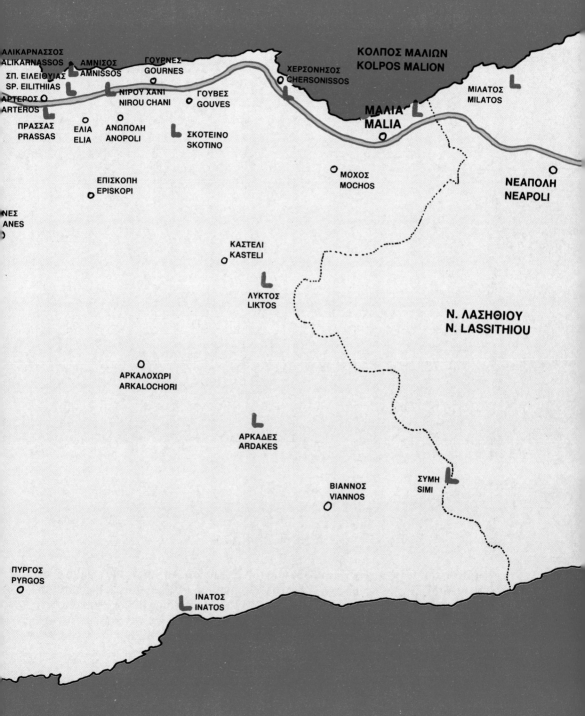

ΚΡΗΤΙΚΟ ΠΕΛΑΓΟΣ
KRITIKO PELAGOS

ΚΟΛΠΟΣ ΜΑΛΙΩΝ
KOLPOS MALION

ΑΛΙΚΑΡΝΑΣΣΟΣ
ALIKARNASSOS
ΑΜΝΙΣΟΣ
AMNISSOS
ΓΟΥΡΝΕΣ
GOURNES
ΧΕΡΣΟΝΗΣΟΣ
CHERSONISSOS
ΜΙΛΑΤΟΣ
MILATOS
ΣΠ. ΕΙΛΕΙΘΥΙΑΣ
SP. EILITHIIAS
ΝΙΡΟΥ ΧΑΝΙ
NIROU CHANI
ΓΟΥΒΕΣ
GOUVES
ΑΡΤΕΡΟΣ
ARTEROS
ΜΑΛΙΑ
MALIA
ΠΡΑΣΣΑΣ
PRASSAS
ΕΛΙΑ
ELIA
ΑΝΩΠΟΛΗ
ANOPOLI
ΣΚΟΤΕΙΝΟ
SKOTINO
ΝΕΑΠΟΛΗ
NEAPOLI
ΕΠΙΣΚΟΠΗ
EPISKORI
ΜΟΧΟΣ
MOCHOS
ΝΕΣ
ANES
ΚΑΣΤΕΛΙ
KASTELI
ΛΥΚΤΟΣ
LIKTOS
Ν. ΛΑΣΗΘΙΟΥ
N. LASSITHIOU
ΑΡΚΑΛΟΧΩΡΙ
ARKALOCHORI
ΑΡΚΑΔΕΣ
ARDAKES
ΒΙΑΝΝΟΣ
VIANNOS
ΣΥΜΗ
SIMI
ΠΥΡΓΟΣ
PYRGOS
ΙΝΑΤΟΣ
INATOS

ΛΥΒΙΚΟ ΠΕΛΑΓΟΣ
LIVIKO PELAGOS

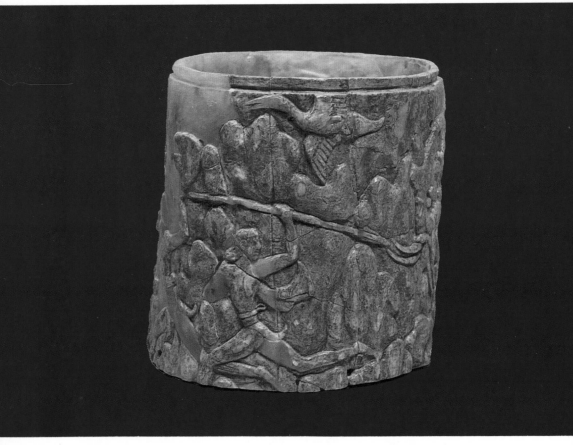

Katsambas: Cemetery. Cylindrical pyxis made from ivory with an engraved image of the capture of a bull.

AMNISSOS

Beyond Katsambas, Alikarnassos and the Heraclion Airport is the small valley of the river Karteros which was known as **"Omphalion Pedion"** during the antiquity while the river was named **Amnissos and Triton.** According to the myth the umbilical cord of the infant Zeus fell here when his mother Rhea was carrying him to the Idean Cave to hide him. To the north-east of the valley is the hill named **Paleohora,** known earlier as **Messovouni** which was the site of the ancient city of **Amnissos.**

According to the tradition Amnissos was one of the ports used by the inhabitants of Knossos. On a tablet written in linear B and found in Knossos it is stated that Amnissos is a "pot of honey" to Eileithyia.

Amnissos: Villa of the Lillies

The monuments to be visited in the area include the **villa of the lillies** on the eastern side of the hill, the **Sanctuary of Zeus Thenatas** on the west, the **Cave of Eileithyia,** where the cult rituals of the cult took place, at a distance of 500m to the south of the hill and on the south side of the valley the **Minoan villa at Prassas.**

A) THE VILLA OF THE LILLIES

It was excavated in 1932 by Professor S. Marinatos and studied by Professor N. Platon. The external walls of the villa were built with hewn porous stone-blocks on which the trident and star symbols were carved. The villa was destroyed around 1500 BC either by an earthquake or a tidal wave. On its NE corner it has a room

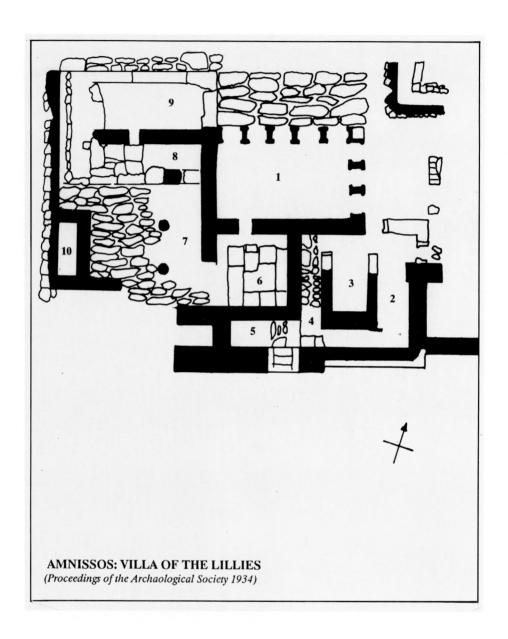

AMNISSOS: VILLA OF THE LILLIES
(Proceedings of the Archaological Society 1934)

with many doors and to the north there is a collonade. Further the villa had a bathroom which had an entry through a small stairway (3) while the ruins of another stairway (5) hint that there was a second floor. The villa was built with porolith, sand and limestone. The enchanting frescoes of lillies found lent the name to the villa. The frescoes are in white and red colours and decorate the front of the buildings. Among other artifacts found in the villa there are clay potteries of the marine style.

Amnissos: Temple of Zeus Thenatas. Eagle made of porous stone, 7th cent. B.C.

13

Amnissos: The Cave of Eileithyia

Amnissos: The fresco of the lillies, 16th cent. B.C.

B) THE TEMPLE OF ZEUS THENATAS

The temple was also excavated by Professor S. Marinatos. The dedication of the sanctuary to Zeus is related to the myth of the umbilical cord while the word **Thenatas** derives from **Thenai,** the city located her in the historic period. The sanctuary is an open enclosure with a large altar for pyres and sacrifices. The sanctuary was founded in the Minoan era, as it witnessed by the lower part of its eastern large wall which is built of huge porous stone-blocks bearing engraved symbols. The wall was supplemented in height during the geometric period (900-700 BC) and it was used in later periods as well. The steps on the northern part of the wall look very much alike to the stone seats of the theater grounds of the Minoan palaces.

An interesting item found in the sanctuary are two life-sized sitting eagles made of porous stone and dating from the 7th century BC. The eagle is, of course, the symbol of Zeus. The worship of Jezus at this sanctuary continued until the end of the antique era. Several of the inscriptions at the sanctuary give important historical information, as for instance the name of the heroic general Lastenes who fought the Romans.

CAVE OF EILEITHYIA AT AMNISSOS
(drawing by EL. PLATAKIS)

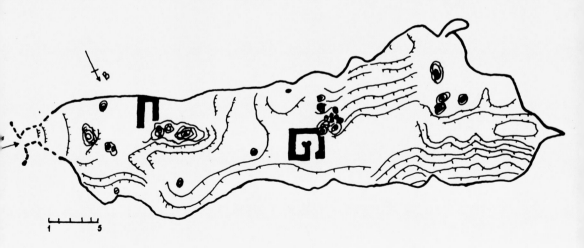

C) THE CAVE OF EILEITHYIA

This cave was discovered by accident approximately 100 years ago and was known as **Neraidospilios** or **Spilios tis Koutsouras.** The first excavation was undertaken by I. Hadzidakis while Professor S. Marinatos completed the works in 1929.

Homer mentions the cave in his works and is considered to be the most sacred and famous cave in Crete. The use of the cave for worship was of very long duration starting at the end of the neolithic period (3000 BC) and ending in the 6th or 7th century AD. Here the adoration of the great Minoan goddess worshipped in her chtonic aspect is succeeded during the historic period by the Goddess of childbirth, Eileithya, a daughter of Zeus and Hera born in this cave according to Pausanias. The stalactites in this cave were considered sacred and were enclosed with a low wall in a holy temple.

The entrance to the cave, marked by a fig tree faces the east as most of the holy caves.

The cave has a length of 60m, a width of 9 to 12m and a height of 3 to 5m. To the left of the entrance are some ruins of a rectangular edifice. The stalagmites in the center of the cave were considered to represent a woman with her child on her side. Offers of milk and honey we presented to these stalagmites which were enclosed in a temple. The neolithic pottery found is of remarkable quality while the finds include also potteries from the Minoan and historic eras. Outside the cave there is the "square of the altars" where worshipping ceremonies took place. Nearby were also the houses of the priests.

PRASSAS

A few decades ago N. Platon excavated a country villa remarkably preserved near the village of Prassas. The walls remain intact from the basement to the roof. Its locations is excellent with a splendid view on the Karteros valley and the Sea of Crete.

NIROU KHANI

The road from Amnissos continues over Kakon Oros descending to Pachia Ammos and to the area Vatheianos Kambos or Almyrides where the fast-growing settlement of Kokkini Khani is located. In 1918 S. Xanthoudidis excavated here the first known large Minoan **Megaron** (Mansion) situated in the center of a settlement which continued to the seashore, where, near the church of Aghii Theodori ruins of the port facilities have been found.

MEGARON NIROU
(Αρχαιολογική Εφημερίς, 1922, π. 3)

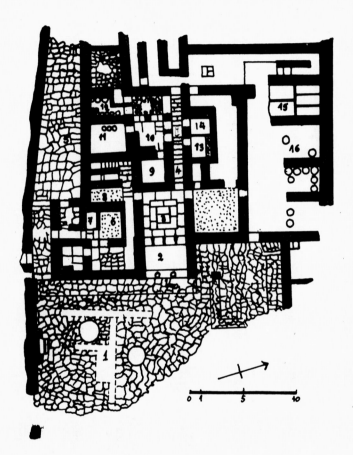

MEGARON NIROU

MEMORANDUM

1. Eastern Court
2. Entrance
3. Hall
4. Corridor
5. Southern Court
6. Sanctuary of the Axes
7. The Grate
8. The Room of the Lamp
9. The Room of the Lamps
10. The Room of the Benches
11. The storage room of the altars
12. The storage room of the altars
13. The room with the bench
14. The room of the three altars
15. Granaries
16. Oil and wine storage rooms

Nirou Khani, Megaron: The sanctuary with the grate.

Nirou Khani, Megaron: Internal corridor

Nirou Khani, Megaron: Room with wide bench.

Nirou Khani, Megaron. East Court.

Nirou Khani: Megaron, general view from the N.W.

Nirou Khani, Megaron: Built altar on the East Court.

*Nirou Khani, Megaron.
Cylindrical clay vase of
the Marine style. 16th
cent. B.C.*

*Nirou Khani, Megaron.
Stone lamp, 16th cent. BC*

A) THE MEGARON

The Megaron which had two storeys and a nice view to the sea is built with palatial splendour with large hewn stones on the outside while unwrought stones, unbaked clay and straw or seaweed were used on the inside. In addition the internal sides had been covered with wooden frames and plaster. The roof, doors and window frames were wooden, the prints of wich can be seen. Most of the walls were covered with limestone plaster tiles. The Megaron was destroyed by a fire the heat of which turned the stone into lime and baked the clay. The most important parts of the Megaron are described below:

The **east court** (1) is paved with flagstones. To the south a dais with steps was built which bore a pair of "horns of concecration" made of stone. Ceremonies took place in this court. A narrower paved court lies to the south of the Megaron (5). The **entrance** (2) to the Megaron was on the eastern side through a portico formed by two columns followd by a room with many doors which lead into the main hall (3) which communicated through three doors with other parts of the Megaron. A long corridor (4) divides the Megaron into two wings. There is a further part in the north side which included the storage rooms for grain (15), oil and wine (16).

Of interest are the rooms with the built-in benches made of gypsum (10, 13) as well as those where the stone lamps have been found. Also the rooms in which coated clay tripod altars have been found are worth visiting.

The sanctuary of the Megaron (6) had a built-in grate (7) in its southwest corner. Four large bronze axes, the largest ever found, were in this sanctuary.

According to the excavator, S. Xanthoudidis, and also to A. Evans, the Megaron was the seat of a sovereign bearing the title of Archpriest. This is substantiated by the many artifacts destined to worship which were found here: altars, axes, double horns of consecration.

B) THE HARBOUR OF AGHII THEODORI

The ruins of the ancient harbour lie at a distance of a 1km. northwest of the Megaron, near the church of Aghii Theodori. The Minoan settlement was in the same area. S. Xanthoudidis and S. Marinatos brought to light many buildings, storage rooms, houses, and a rectangular enclosure. Near the seafornt there is a man-made rectangular cavity hewn in the rock which is considered to be the shipyard used by the Minoans to built their ships.

Nirou Khani, Megaron: Room with plaster benches.

Nirou Khani: Entrance and many-doored megaron

Nirou Khani, Megaron: Room with pillaster.

GOURNES - GOUVES

In the area of the Gournes village I. Hadzidakis excavated in 1914 5 tombs dating from the end of the pre-palatial period and belonging to a Minoan settlement nearby. The tombs comprised a complex of rectangular burial halls and a depository pit. The graves contained approx. 30 bodies and over 100 small clay veses, mainly small prochoe, a stone vase, clay figurines, seals, necklaces, and scarabs. The form of the rectangular burial structures was common mainly in the eastern and northern Crete during the prepalatial and early palatial periods.

A Minoan settlement and a cemetery of the neopalatial period was excavated on the beach of the village Gouves.

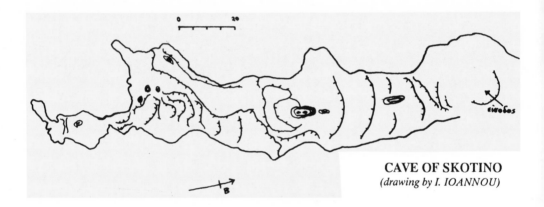

CAVE OF SKOTINO
(drawing by I. IOANNOU)

SKOTINO

The sacred ritual cave, known currently as the Cave of Aghia Paraskevi, is situated at a distance of 1500m NW of the village of the same name on a 230m high hillock. Its total length is 170m and it covers in total a surface of 2500 sq. m. The average width of the cave is 40m while the maximum height is 47m. According to P. Fauvre who studied it, it is composed of 4 layers. The cave was created by landslides caused by earthquakes.

The cave was known during the Venetian years. It was excavated in 1962 by K. Davaras. The finds include pottery shards dating from the Minoan to the Roman periods as well as lambs and needles made of bone. Three ritual idols of copper in a posture of prayer with their right hands touching their foreheads stand out.

The spelaeologists divided the cave into areas with distinctive and characteristics names: Entrance, Great Temple, Altars, Sanctuary, Chambers of Worship, Chamber of Prayer, Chapel. Many stalactites and stalagmites resemble human or animal figures: The Bear, the Head, the Sitting Dog, The Face of the Goddess, the Child's Head. The mineral decoration of the cave is rich, spectacular and glorious.

The Skotino cave was a place of worship from the start of the palaeopalatial period until the end of antiquity. According to P. Fauvre, the young Minoan Goddess Vritomartis (sweet virgin) was worshipped here; he further considers that the cave of Skotino was the famous Labyrinth of Knossos. Next to the entrance of the cave a ruined church dating from the 16th century AD indicates the continuation of worship of the Christian God in an ancient cult site.

Skotino: The cave of worship. Stalagmite in the shape of a "Bear"

Skotino: Cave of worship. Copper statuette of a worshipper.

Skotino: Cave of worship. Copper statuette of a worshipper.

Skotino: Cave of worship. Copper statuette of a worshipper. 16th cent. B.C.

Chersonessos: Marble statue of a "peploforos" (veiled) lady, 2th cent. A.D.

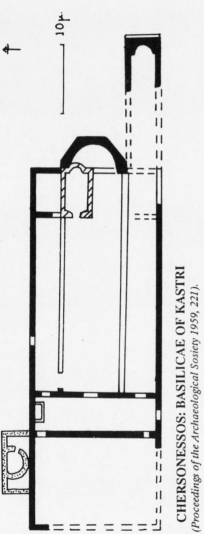

CHERSONESSOS: BASILICAE OF KASTRI
(Proceedings of the Archaeological Sosiety 1959, 221).

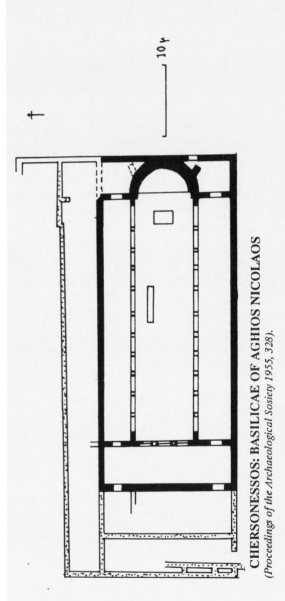

CHERSONESSOS: BASILICAE OF AGHIOS NICOLAOS
(Proceedings of the Archaeological Sosiety 1955, 328).

CHERSONESSOS

A) THE TOWN

After the visit of the Skotino cave, the tour continues eastward to the resort Chersonessos (harbour) which is built on the same site as the ancient town of Chersonessos that flourished during the Roman and early Byzantine periods.

Strabo mentions that accordint to the tradition the town was founded at this location by the Tyrrhenians who brought along a wooden idol of the goddess Vri-

Chersonessos: General view of the harbour.

tomartis, consequently the patron goddess of the town, in which a splendid temple was dedicated to her. It is considered that Chersonessos served for a time as the port of the great ancient city of the Lyctos plain, although at other periods it was an independent city with own monetary units. During the early Christian and Protobyzantine periods it was the seat of a bishop founded by Apostle Titus.

The excavated ruins at the site of Poli date from various periods and include the man-made jetty and the fishtanks, the theatre, the fountain and the Basilicae as well as the Acropolis situated on the small peninsula Kastri, the town's aqueduct that brought the water from the plain and a part of which remains at Xerokomares, on the road to Kastelli Pediadas and Lassithi.

B) THE THEATRE

Only the wallbuttress and the concavity survive from the ancient theatre of Chersonessos which was built of bricks and plaster. The walls are 0,70m thick and preserved to a height of 3m. The internal concavity diameter is 33m. Behind the curved wall are the fundaments of the external arches of the building. No other ruin is visible and the representation of the ancient theater by O. Belli does not reflect reality. Possibly, future excavations will bring to light other interesting ruins. It is though certain that the theatre was situated onm the southeastern side of the town in the vicinity of other large public buildings.

C) THE FOUNTAIN

The low pyramidal fountain is situated on the coast, near the site where the ancient jetty is visible under the water. Every side measures 2,5m in length while the height is 0,75m. All four sides of the fountain are decorated with multicoloured mosaics which are preserved well only on one side. The items represented on the mosaics include marine and coastal scenes with fishermen, boats, fish, sea-birds (ducks) and land animals (goats) and are surrounded by a multicoloured mosaic frame.

D) THE BASILICAE

The three large Basilicae excavated so far by A. Orlandos in 1955-59 and by the Archaeological Authorities recently, witness the prosperity and importance of the peninsula during the Paleochristian and Protobyzantine periods. The first Basilica is situated on the peninsula of Kastri, the second near the chapel of Aghios Nicholaos and the third, recently excavated, is in the southern part of the Paleochristian sector of the town.

Chersonessos: Fountain of the Roman years with mosaic representations

Chersonessos: Protobyzantine basilicae of Kastri

Chersonessos: Basilicae of Kastri. Mosaic floor

Chersonessos: Basilicae of Aghios Nikolaos. Mosaic floor.

Chersonessos: Protobyzantine Basilicae of Aghios Nikolaos

Aerial Photograph of Chersonessos.

Design of the golden handle of the sword of Malia.

MALIA

A) Geography, topography, mythology

The small coastal plain of Malia is situated in the northeastern part of the Pediada-District of the Heraclion-Province, and spread from the northern side of the Dicte mountain range to the sea. On the eastern side of the plain stand the ruins of one of the most important Minoan cities that flourished on the second millenium BC along with the other great cities of Knossos, Phaestos, Aghia Triada, Archanes, Zakros, Paleokastro, Gournia and Kommos.

The very fertile plain of Malia has a very important agricultural production including bananas, olive-oil and flowers. The natural flora around the archaeological sites includes carob trees, wild olive trees, lentisks and various bushes.

The Minoan city had founded on a strategic point in the centre of the ancient road that connecting central and eastern Crete, approx. in the same area of the current road from Heraclion to Aghios Nikolaos. The plain of Malia is also the natural exit to the sea from the plain of Lassithi.

After the modern town of Malia which is one of the most developed areas in tourism in Crete the road continues through the very green plain to the low and picturesque hill of Profitis Elias at a distance of 300m of which are the ruins of the ancient Minoan palace and the Minoan city.

The myth of Sarpedon, one of the best known Cretan myths, is linked to the city of Malia. Sarpedon was, according to the the myth, the third brother of Minos and Rhadamanthys. Minos clashed with him and exiled him together with his friend Miletos to Asia Minor where he became the king of Lycia and an ally of the Trojans during the Trojan war, while Miletos founded the city of Miletos in Karia which was, thus, a colony of the Cretan city Milatos. This myth echoes the real geographical expansion of the Cretans during the height of the Minoan civilization and this is corroborated by the archaeological finds in Miletos of Asia Minor.

Prof. S. Marinatos assumed, based on this myth, that Sarpedon ruled at Malia as Rhadamanthys at Phaestos and certainly Minos at Knossos. Other researchers maintain that the ancient name of the city was Tarmaros, a name found in an area nearby and associated to the Termiles, a people of of Asia Minor and the names of places Termeros and Termissos in the same area.

The name Malia derives from the recent Venetian period and originates from the adjectives **omalos - omalion** meaning level, smooth.

B) An account of the archaeological research

The first known ancient artifacts from the area of Malia were some goldleaves found in the Elliniko Leivadi are as noted the English Admiral Spratt in the mid-19th century. Copper cauldrons and clay sarcophagi were found accidentally on the coast at the beginning of the 20th century in 1915 Hadzidakis began the excavations on the hillock Azymo financed by the Archaeological Society. He discovered half of the western wing of the palace as well as various along the coast.

He proposed to cooperate with the French Archaeological School who accepted, but undertook the excavations by themselves as Hadzidakis became ill meanwhile. These excavations started in 1921 and are continued to this day with some interruptions. They are taking place in the area of the palace, in the sectors of the city, in the cemeteries on the coast situated at Aletrouvopetra, Chryssolakkos and the islets Christos and Aghia Varvara.

Reports of the excavations as well as other staduies were published by the French Archaeological School as "Etudes Crétoises" as from 1928. The final compound publication was in 1980 by H. Van Effenterre.

Malia, Palace: Slanted building

Malia, Palace: The "Loggia"

Reconstruction of the palace of Malia from N.W. (after Graham).

Malia, Palace: Theater grounds

Malia, Palace: North portico of the central court.

Malia, Palace: The sanctuary of the pillasters

Malia: Prepalatial libation vessel in the shape of a goddess. 2000 B.C.

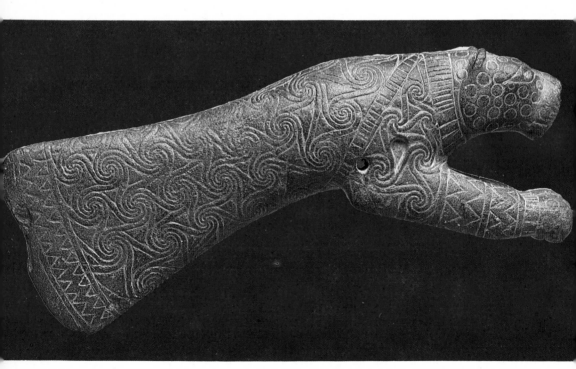

Malia, Palace: The head of a scepter, made from slate, in the image of a Leopard and an axe. 17th cent. B.C.

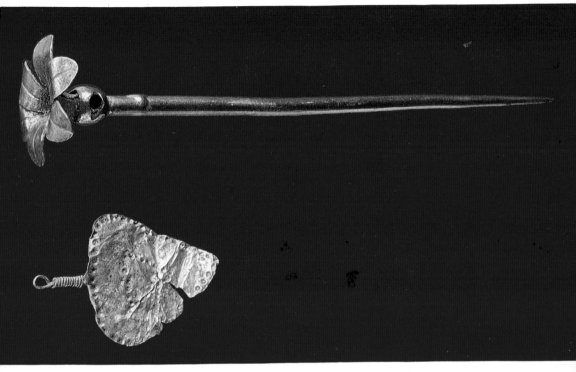

*Malia, Chrysolakkos: Gold jewelry, brooch with flower-shaped head
and heart-shaped amulet 19th cent. B.C.*

*Malia, Palace: Golden sheathing of a sword handle with the image
of an acrobat. 17th cent. B.C.*

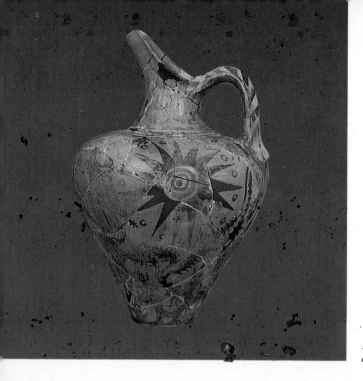

Malia: Aerial photograph of the archaeological site.

Malia: Prepalatial prochoe of the basilica style. 2400 B.C.

C) A brief history

1) The oldest period of Cretan history, the neolithic period, is very little represented in Malia. Only very few discoveries from the palace area (pieces of pottery made of clay) witness the presence of humanity in the area.

A continuous, important and vigorous presence of human activity in Malia is noted as from the middle of the 3rd millenium BC, during the proto-Minoan II period (2500-2200 BC) and continues without interruption until the end of prehistory, as proven by excavations and the recent study of archaeological data. The houses of the prepalatial settlement (2500-2000 BC) were located in many sites in the deeper stata south of the palace. Clay pottery of royal style with spotted surface witness the close relationship with the important centers of eastern Crete in the same period. Better known are the tombs of the prepalatial period which were hewn in the rocky soil at a distance of approx. 500m north of the palace near the sea. These tombs included finds of clay and stone vessels and well as some jewelry.

2) Towards to the end of the 3rd millenium, around 2000 BC, an economically and culturally developed settlement exists in Malia which developed further into a palatial city, simultaneously with the other palatial centers at Knossos and Phaestos. Several local peculiarites led to conflicting assumptions regarding the chronology of the foundation, the duration and destruction of the old and the new palaces. The chronology suggested by N. Platon is followed here as it is very hard to identify the sections of the old palace. The chronology of the northwestern segment of the old palace (marked white on the plan) is, however, certain. The same applies for the East Storage Rooms, according at least according to the French archaeologists.

The problem of the chronology of the old palace occured due to the lack of any large quantity of vaulted ceramics of good quality found in Malia, which characterise the old palaces at Knossos and Phaestos. Therefore the palace of Malia is generally considered as more provincial than the two other great palatial centers.

However, the period of the old palace, is well known in Malia through the many excavated houses in various sectors around the palace. In certain cases the discoveries are unique and include the only known seal-making workshop as well as a temple of the same period. The unique **agora** of Malia is dated from this period also as well as the cemetery of Chrysolakkos.

3) The old palace was destroyed approx. at 1700 BC along with the other great palaces. However, it was rebuilt in the same location with basically the same plan. The first building phase of the new palace was in the 17th century BC. To this phase belongs the strata which contained the golden royal swords. Some changes in the plan of the palace occured after 1600 BC, the multidoored Megaron was built while the area of the central court in the western wing was reduced. This palace of the second and third neopalatial phase is that surviving today with the exceptions mentioned.

The destruction of the new palace occured simultaneously with that of the other palaces at approx. 1450 BC. It is assumed that Malia was inhabited again during the 14th and 13th century BC and that the small slanting building dates from this period.

4) The last ruins of the antiquity in the area of Malia are situated at Marmara, approx. 500m. northwest of the palace, near the coast. It is an early Christian Basilicae dating from the 6th century AD with partly excavated mosaic floors. In front of the arch of the Basilicae a burial caverna was discovered it containing a huge marble sarcophagus with beautiful engravings on its cover (today it is in the hall of sculpture in the Museum of Heraclion). The sarcophagus dates from the period of the Antonini (second half of the 2nd century AD) or the 3rd century AD, but it was used again in the early Christian period. Many researchers place a city of the historic years in the same area where the early Christian Basilica is, a city with the assumed name of Arsinoe but this is not corraborated by any data. Nevertheless, there are, extensive ruins of a settlement dating from the Roman period (2nd-3d century AD) in the area of this Basilicae.

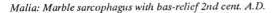

Malia: Marble sarcophagus with bas-relief 2nd cent. A.D.

D) Visit of the site

The French excavators of Malia have characterised the main compartment of the palace with Latin letters, the rooms in each compartment with Arabic numbers while the houses and sectors of the city were given Greek capital letters. The same excavators were given certain distinctive names to sections or compartments that present a great interest. Here a simpler numbering system is followed with Arab numbers specifying the order in which the visitor is likely to visit the various compartments, rooms, sectors, houses etc. For a better understanding though, the distinctive names given and established by the excavators are also maintained. The duration of the visit is approx. 45 minutes for the palace while further 45 minutes for the visit of the houses and the cemetery are required. The idea of the civilization of Malia is completed, however, only in the Heraclion Museum, where the treasures of Malia are exhibited.

Malia, Palace: Copper prochoe. 16th cent. B.C.

Malia, Palace: Copper basin. 16th cent. B.C.

Malia, Palace: West Great Staircase

Malia, Palace: The circular "Kernos"

Malia, Palace: The Road of the sea

A) THE PALACE

The Minoan palace of Malia has many resemblances with the palaces of Knossos, Phaestos and Zakros and of course, its own particularities as it was considered to be poorer and more provincial than those mentioned above. Ressembling are the two great courts central and west, while compared to the palace of Knossos it has a similar arrangement of rooms and sections in the west wing where the throne room of Malia, the Central Sanctuary and the West Storage rooms are. Compared to the palace of Phaestos the Multidoored Megaron has the same location in the northwest sector. With the palace in Zakros it shares the location of the Hall with Columns in the northern sector.

The basic difference in the palace of Malia is the existence of the East Storage Rooms and that of five more Storage Room complex in other parts of the palace. Also unique are the Granaries and the Altar in the centre of the Central Court.

The peculiarities of the palace of Malia are also to be seen in the building materials used. The alabaster and plaster of the other great palaces which lend them their bright appearance are not found in Malia. Here humbler local materials have been used as ammouda (sandstone), sideropetra (ironstone) and the unbaked plinths made of clay and seaweeds. The walls were of course covered by thick coats of plaster and often painted red.

The palace of Malia has 3 entrances. The most notable were the South Entrance and the North Entrance, while the third, was a secondary entrance to the east side. The city's main roads ended at each entrance. The Harbour Road connected the palace with the Agora and ended at the North Entrance.

The palace had also two paved external courts on the west and south as well as three inner courts, the also paved Central Court as well as two further small ones, the Court of the Tower and the North Court both of which were paved. The courts and their uses will be mentioned further below, during the visit of the palace.

(1) WEST COURT-SOUTH SECTION-WEST WING

From the paved **West Court (1)** which is traversed by the procession roads which constitute part of the city's network, the visitor arrives to the southeastern corner of the Court where the eight cyclical **Granaries (2)** are. They were circural roofed constructions as it proven by the remaining central pillar that supported the roofs. There is also the assumption that they were used as water cisterns.

Continuing to the south outside the palace into the south court one reaches the **South Sanctuary (3)** which has an external entrance and a room with a stone bench and an altar on which clay vessels and other artifacts were found. The **South Entrance (4)** wide and paved, leads straight to the **Central Court (11)** from the south. To the west of the entrance the famous **Kernos (5)** is situated. It is a low round stone with many small cavities on its circumference and a larger cavity in its center. On this altar took place the **panspermia** ceremony, the offering of various seeds and fruits to the gods to be blessed, a custom preserved in the Christian religion.

*Malia, Palace: Outdoor sanctuary with a circular
"Kernos" for offerings.*

Malia, Palace: South entrance

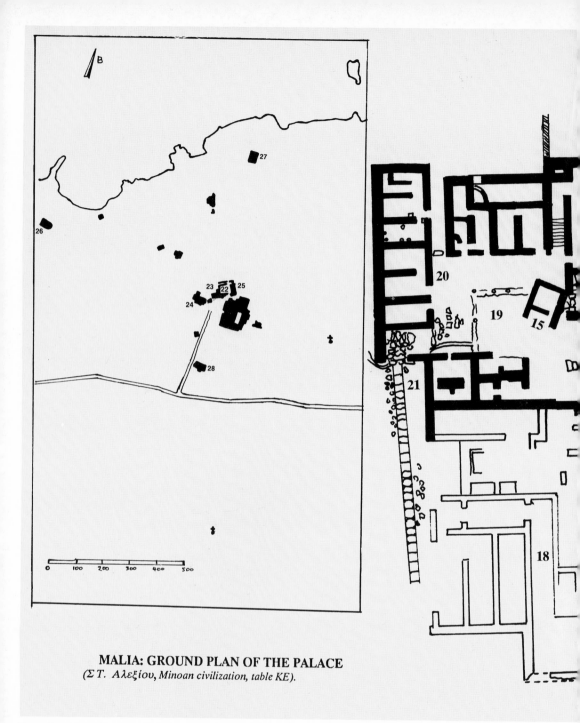

MALIA: GROUND PLAN OF THE PALACE
(Σ Τ. Αλεξίου, Minoan civilization, table KE).

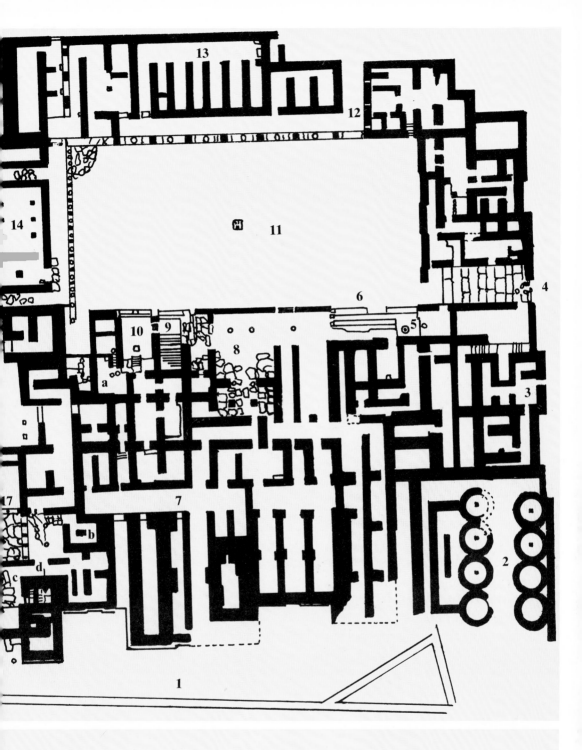

Near Kernos and to the north are the **Theater Grounds (6)** a wide stone stair-case with the same use to that of the similar grounds of the palaces of Knossos and Phaestos. The spectators sitting here could watch the ceremonies that took place in the Central Court.

The west wing of the palace of Malia is divided into three main compartments, the Central Sanctuary, the Loggia and the West. Storage Rooms which were used for separate but combined functions:

The **West Storage Rooms (7)** occupy the western half of the west wing. These are long narrow rooms spreading west of a corridor on a north-south axe. Pieces of earthen casks and many clay pots for domestic use have been found here.

The central part of the west wing consists of the complex of the **Central San-**

Malia, Palace: Circular granaries

cturary (8). The core of the sanctuary is the room with the two pillars, on which holy symbols are engraved. In front of the crypt with the pillars is the ante-chamber with a bench, open to the side of the Central Court.

The floor of the Sanctuary is paved with flagstones and its walls were coated in red dye. In a smaller room west of the crypt with the pillars there is another bench and a coated pit contained burned bones, remains of sacrifices. The Sanctuary communicated with the West Storage Rooms as in the palace of Knossos.

North of the Sanctuary is the **Great Staircase (9)** which led from the Central Court to the upper floor of the west wing of the palace. This staircase connected with the Loggia from the north and with a paved room as well as with the ante-chamber of the Sanctuary from the south. The complex of the **Loggia (10)** has in

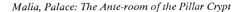

Malia, Palace: The Ante-room of the Pillar Crypt

the palace of Malia the same location as the complex of the Throne Room at Knossos. The Loggia was a covered area slightly higher than the Central Court. It had two collumns on its west side and and altar in its center. It would seem that the King-Priest worshipped while the crowd watched the ceremony from the Central Court. Northwest of the Loggia is a smaller **room (10a)** in which important find were made including the stone scepter shaped like an axe and the head of a leopard both in cask as well as a digger and the amazing long sword with a stone handle covered in gold while the ball-formed tip of the handle was made of crystal. The French excavators named this sword Durendal after Roland's famed sword. In this room the preparation of the king for the sacrificial ceremonies took place, while also the holy vessels were stored here.

Malia, Palace: Part of the west wing

Malia, Palace: West Court

Malia, Palace: West Wing

(2) CENTRAL COURT - EAST WING

The **Central Court (11)** of the palace of Malia is a rectangular, are paved with flagstones with a north-south axe. The flagstones remain only in a few spots. In the north and east side were porticos which were composed alternatively rows of columns and pillars which separated the courts by low walls and fences. In the center of the Court and exactly opposite the Central Sanctuary is the Altar which was grate-shaped and on which the sacrifices was made.

At the south end of the eastern portico is the **East Entrance (12)** of the palace, a corridor that led straight into the Central Court. North of this entrance is the Eastern wing which housed the **East Storage Rooms (13)** a total of six long and narrow rooms which spread west from a long corridor. In these storage rooms the casks stood in two long lines along the walls while in the centre of each room the floor formed a drainage ditch ending in a collector at the western end of the ro-

Malia, Palace: The North Court

om. The long corridor of the storage rooms had a low parapet to the east on which caskets were placed. These storage rooms were designed for liquids as can be deduced by the existing drainage system and the ditches. Today they are off limits to the visitors.

(3) NORTH SECTOR-MULTIDOORED MEGARON

To the north of the northern portico of the central Court is the great **Collumned Hall (14)** which is composed by an antechamber with a central pillar and a large room whose roof of which was supported by two of three pillars. The use of this hall is still unknown, it may have been a kitchen area for the banquet hall which would have been on the upper floor. Also, it may have been used for some kind of religious ceremonies.

West of the collumned Hall is a paved corridor which connects the Central and

Malia, Palace: Antechamber of the sanctuary of the pillasters

North Courts. At the North end of this corridor the **slanting building (15)** is located and has a different orientation than the palace. It is a sanctuary of the metapalatial years which was built by large hewn stones from the ruines of the palace. It is composed by a prodrome between the two gateposts and a square main temple.

East of the "Slanting Building" are granaries and a staircase for the upper floor.

West of the corridor is the **"Court of the Tower" (16)** which took its name from a peculiar room with thick walls which looks like a tower. Its ground floor was used as a storage room for vegetables.

West of the "Court of the Tower" is the **Many-Doored Megaron (17)**, where the

Malia, Palace: East portico of the central court.

king lived. It was composed by the main Megaron and various other interesting rooms around it. North and south of it there were porticos with collonades. Next to the south portico there is a skylight, and further south a significant small room with a central pillar of worship. In this room the record of clay rods, tablets and disks with inscriptions was found, as well as seals for the wooden cases of the records. West of the Megaron is the antechamber of the Purification Cistern. In this Antechamber, the unique "Sword of the Acrobat" was found, with the goldcovered handle on which the dangerous jump of the acrobat is depicted. Another large sword was found with it. The stratum which contained the swords was considered palaeopalatial at first, but possibly it belongs to the first phase of the new palace, in the 17th century B.C.

Malia: Palace. The road of the sea.

Malia, Palace: Central court

Malia, Palace: Many-doored Megaron

Malia, Palace: North paved corridor

Malia, Palace: Collumned Symposium Hall

North of the many-doored building, extensive ruins of the old palace, which had **collonades,** have been uncovered **(18)**.

The visit continues to the "**North Court**" **(19),** which has collonades in its north and east sides. The compartments west of the Court were workshops. To the north and east there are other **storage room complexes (20).** The cask that stands in the north side of the Court is of the neopalatial period. From the North Entrance, the Road of the Sea ends in the northwest corner of the **North Court (21).**

The cask next to the road is of the palaeopalatial period.

From the North Entrance, following the paved road, the visitor comes to an important sector of the Minoan city, which we will see immediately below.

*Malia, Chrysolakkos: Palaeopalatial cemetery with rectangular
burial chambers*

B) THE CITY AND THE CEMETERIES

In the six centuries of the prime of palatial Minoan civilization, an extended city grew and flourished around the palace of Malia; it had an area of about one square kilometer, excepting the cemeteries. To the north, the city spread almost to the sea. From this city, several neighborhoods and single dwellings have been excavated; the civic center of the city was unearthed very near the palace, to the northwest.

A significant network of wide, paved, roads and plazas, many of which have come to light, connect the neighborhoods of the city with the civic center and the palace. At Malia, more than anywhere else, the city planning organization of a minoan city-palace center can be studied. The ceremonial roads of the west court of the palace and the northern "Road of the Sea" are a part of the road network of the city.

The limits of the city are set to the north and east by a long enclosure which was built from large blocks of stone in the palaeopalatial period. This enclosure, according to Prof. Alexiou, could be part of the fortification of the city. The plan of the city, with the streets and plazas, was also organized in the palaeopalatial pe-

Malia, Chrysolakkos: Circular offering table

riod. This existed until the final destruction of the palace and the city around 1450 B.C.

Two temples have been excavated in the southwest part of the city, while there had been another temple on the top of the hill Profitis Elias, about 500m. south of the city.

The cemeteries of Malia are located in a large area at a distance of 500m. from the palace, to the northeast, near the rocky shore. Tombs of many types and periods have been excavated in the locations Aletrouvopetra, Chrysolakkos, isles of Christ and Aghia Varvara, and Aghia Pelagia.

Malia, Chrysolakkos: Palaeopalatial cemetery

The older burials were made in natural cavities of the rocks (Charniers), in the second prepalatial period and until its end, on around 1900 B.C. In the third prepalatial period (2200 - 1900 B.C.) the first burials at Chrysolakkos were made, in a square burial building which continued to be used during the palaeopalatial period and was considered a "royal" cemetery.

(1) THE AGORA - SECTORS D AND M

The paved "Road of the Sea" leads the visitor from the North Entrance of the palace to the **"Agora"** (22) of Malia, a square with an area of 1160 sq.m., larger than the Central Court of the palace (1036 sq.m.) The Agora had a floor of plaster and walls around it. It was founded, as were most of the houses that have be-

Malia, Chrysolakkos: Gold bee pendant 1500 B.C.

Malia: Chryssolakkos: Gold jewelry, 15 cent. B.C.

en uncovered, in the beginning of the palaeopalatial period. The existence of this Agora as a civic and economic center is a unique phenomenon in palaeopalatial Minoan Crete. The corresponding "Agoras" at Gournia and Aghia Triada belong to the neopalatial and metapalatial periods and have a different architectural form.

West of the Agora is the "**Columned Crypt**" **(23),** which is covered under a hangar today. It is a carefully built underground hall with plaster on the walls and benches on the sides. According to Prof. Van Effenterre, it could have been used us a Prytanaeum for meetings.

Further west of the Agora is **Sector D (24),** with the plazas and streets among the houses which are dated to the palaeopalatial period (Db, Dc), while another house, Da, is a typical sample of neopalatial Minoan architecture: it has a many-doored room, a megaron, a purification cistern etc.

Proceeding further west, the visitor comes to **Sector M (25),** with the large houses of the prepalatial period, each of which has many dozens of rooms. The characteristic elements of these houses are the existence of records, which are tablets with hieroglyphics, a seal-making workshop, temples and storage rooms. Streets and small, paved squares are among the houses.

Northwest of the excavation of the Minoan city, and at a distance of 600m from the palace, near the coast, one may visit the **palaeochristian Basilica (26)** from which the large sarcophagus with the engraved images that is in the Heraclion Museum originates. The basilica had been divided into three aisles by interior collonades, with an inscripted Sanctuary niche in a group of rooms ("pastoforia"). There was a mosaic with geometric subjects and three-coloured rosettes on the floor of the central aisle. Of architectural parts, complex capitals to columns of the Ionian style survive. The basilica is dated in the middle of the 6th century A.D., in the reign of the Emperor Justinian.

The ruins of the settlement of late antiquity which existed in the Malia area spread around the ruins of the basilica. The basilica may have been the parish church of this settlement.

(2) THE CEMETERY AT CHRYSOLAKKOS

North of neighborhood A of the city, and until the rocky shore, spread the cemeteries of the city, and among them **Chrysolakkos (27)** stands out. It is a square complex which is composed of a large enclosure, which survives in the north and a little to the east and west, and of a portico to the east, which is formed by a row of pillars. The main building, built with hewn ironstones, is divided into many small rooms-tombs, which could·be reached only from above and were covered with slabs of stone. The court which surrounds the building is paved with flagstones, and under the flagstones the burials which contained the most significant discoveries have been made. At Chrysolakkos survived elements which proved the offering of various objects to the dead: a stone offering table, another offering table made of plaster and an altar.

From Chrysolakkos came not only the sole jewelry of the Heraclion Museum (bee pendant etc) but also the jewels of the "Treasure of Aegina" in the British Museum.

Returning from the visit of the palace, the city, and the cemeteries anyone who wishes may visit **House E (28),** which is located south of the palace and is considered a Lesser Palace: it has porticos, storage rooms, murals, temples, a purification cistern etc. It is dated to the neopalatial period.

MILATOS

After the completion of the visit of the Malia archaeological site, the willing visitor may follow the road to the village Milatos, near the shore of which a neopalatial Minoan settlement has been located, and chambered Minoan graves, which contained burials in sarcophagi have been excavated, both in earlier times and more recently.

The name Milatos (Miletos) is mentioned by Homer; it is pre-hellenic cretan name and is connected to the Cretan hero of the same name, as we saw in the mythology of Malia: but, of more importance, it was the originating Metropolis of the great Greek city of Asia Minor, Miletos.

Malia, Chrysolakkos: External perimeter wall of the cemetery

Malia: Islet of Aghia Varvara. Minoan harbour

Malia, Palace: Old Palace storage jar, about 1800 B.C.

BIBLIOGRAPHY

NIROY KHANI
- Στέφανος Ξανθουδίδης, Μινωικού Μεγάρου Νίρου,
Αρχ. Εφημ. 1922, 1-25
AMNISSOS
- Σπυρίδων Μαρινάτος, Ανασκαφαί Αμνισού,
Πρ. Αρχ. Ετ. 1932, 76· 1933, 92 - 100 - 1934, 128-133
SKOTINO
- Paul Faure, Grottes Crétoises,
B.C.H. LXXX, 96
- Paul Faure, Spéléologie et Topographie Crétoises,
BCH LXXXII, 508
- Κωστής Δαβάρας,
BCH, 93 (1969), 620 ff.
- Tyree Loeta, Cretan Sacred Caves,
20ff, Michigan, 1975
- Στυλιανός Αλεξίου,
Αρχ. Δελτ. 18 (1963), Β, 312
- Στυλιανός Αλεξίου,
Κρητ. Χρον. 17 (1963), 398
CHERSONESSOS
- Αναστάσιος Ορλάνδος, Ανασκαφή Βασιλικής Α Χερσονήσου,
Π.Α.Ε. 1955, 328
- Αναστάσιος Ορλάνδος, Ανασκαφή Χερσονήσου Κρήτης,
Π.Α.Ε. 1959, 221
- Ian Sanders, Roman Crete,
95-101, 144-146, Warminsten 1982.

MALIA
1. H. Van Effenterre
Le Palais de Malia et la Cité Minoenne,
2. H. Van Effenterre - Cl. Tire
Guide des Fouilles Françaises en Créte
Paris 1978

3. Στ. Αλεξίου
Μινωικός πολιτισμός με οδηγό των ανακτόρων.
Ηράκλειο, 1964.
4. G. Cadogan
The palaces of Minoan Crete
London 1976
5. W. Graham
The palaces of Crete
New York 1972
6. F. Chapoutièr, etc...
Palais de Malia. Ier - 4 ème Rapports
Etudes Crétoises 1928-62
7. P. Demargne - H. Van Effenterre
Nécropoles de Malia, Ier - 2ème fascicule
Etudes Crétoises 1945, 1963
8. P. Demargne etc...
Maisons de Mallia, Ier - 4 éme fascicule
Etudes Crétoises 1954 - 1976
9. H. Van Effenterre - M. - Cl. Amouretti
Le Centre politique, Ier - 2ème fascicules
10. R. Treuil
Mallia, Sondages au Sud - Quest du Palais
Etudes Crétoises 1975
11. L. Godart - J. P. Olivier
Recueil des Inscriptions en Linéaire A
Etudes Crétoises, vol. 1, 3, 1976
12. R. Joly
Deux larnakes trouvés a Mallia
BCH 1928, 148-157
13. R. Joly
La Salle Hypostule du Palais de Mallia
BCH 1928, 324-346
14. Ν. Πλάτων
Συγκριτική Χρονολογία των Τριών Μινωικών
Ανακτόρων, ΚΡ. ΧΡ.1961,2, 127-136
15. Α. Ζώης
Προβλήματα Χρονολογίας της Μινωικής
Κεραμικής, Β.Α.Ε. 1969
16. Σπ. Μαρινάτος
Les légendes royales de la Créte minoenne
Rev. Arch. 1949 II, 5-18
17. H. Gallet de Santerre
Mallia, aperçy historique
Gr. Chr. 1949, 363-391